Power Distribution Unit (PDU) Secrets

What Everyone Who Works In A Data Center Needs To Know!

"Practical, proven techniques that will help you to make your data center more successful "

Dr. Jim Anderson

Published by:

Blue Elephant Consulting
Tampa, Florida

Printed in the United States of America

Library of Congress Control Number: 2013917838

ISBN-13: 978-1492838470
ISBN-10:1492838470

Warning – Disclaimer

The purpose of this book is to educate and entertain. This book does not promise or guarantee that anyone following the ideas, tips, suggestions, techniques or strategies will be successful. The author, publisher and distributor(s) shall have neither liability nor responsibility to anyone with respect to any loss or damage caused, or alleged to be caused, directly or indirectly by the information contained in this book.

Acknowledgements

Any book like this one is the result of years of real-world work experience. In my over 25 years of working for 7 different firms, I have met countless fantastic people and I've been mentored by some truly exceptional ones. Although I've probably forgotten some of the people who made me the person that I am today, here is my attempt to finally give them the recognition that they so truly deserve:

- Thomas P. Anderson
- Art Puett
- Bobbi Marshall
- Bob Boggs

Dr. Jim Anderson

This book is dedicated to my wife Lori. None of this would have been possible without her love and support.

Thanks for the best 21 years of my life (so far)…!

Speaking.   Negotiating.   Managing.   Marketing.

Table Of Contents

Why Write A Book About PDUs?

Power Distribution Units (PDUs) – you mean power strips, right? That's what I thought when I was first introduced to this product. Boy oh boy was I wrong! Yes, the PDUs that are manufactured to be sold to the owners and operators of data centers do bear some similarities to the simple power strips that we all use at home. But we are really talking about two very different products here.

How much money do you think that a data center operator has invested in just one of the racks of computers that sits in his or her data center? There is the cost of the rack, of course, but then there's the cost of each of the servers that has been plugged into that rack, the networking gear, and the power distribution system. Not to mention the overhead of cooling and power distribution to the rack. Very quickly the value of a single rack can reach US$500,000.

Clearly it's in the best interests of the data center operator to know exactly what is going on with their investment. Questions that need to be answered include how much power is being used, if there is currently a fire, are there any hot spots, and whether there are any liquids in the area.

The problem with today's modern data center is that all too often the answers to these questions are not available unless staff are sent out on to the data center floor with tools to make measurements. This means that a lot could go on when nobody was looking.

Today's modern PDUs do so much more than just simply deliver power to the computers that have been plugged into a rack. They provide the "eyes and ears" that data center operators need in order to determine what is happening with their racks. Modern PDUs can support multiple types of sensors that can be used to piggy-back environmental information along with power usage information back to a central control system.

Sophisticated Data Center Infrastructure Management (DCIM) software applications promise to be able to monitor all aspects of a data center. However, they are expensive and require an additional investment to both install and then maintain. The use of PDUs to collect needed data center status information provides a simple and low cost way to automate the monitoring of a modern data center.

This book has been written to provide you with the information that you'll need in order to compare and contrast different types of PDUs. These sophisticated tools can be difficult to tell apart. This book will look at the features that you really needs and explain how you would use then in the real-world environment of a modern data center.

It is my hope that after having read this book, you'll have the knowledge that you'll need to go out and select the type of PDU that best meets the needs of your business. Once you've done this, you can then implement a solution that will allow you to always know what is going on in your data center.

Good luck!

- Dr. Jim Anderson, October, 2013

About The Author

I must confess that I never set out to be a power distribution unit expert. When I went to school, I studied Computer Science and thought that I'd get a nice job programming and that would be that. Well, at least part of that plan worked out!

My first job was working for Boeing on their F/A-18 fighter jet program. I spent my days programming fighter jet software in assembly language and I loved it. The U.S. government decided to save some money and went looking for other countries to sell this plane to. This put me into an unfamiliar role: I started to meet with foreign military officials and I ended up having to design and implement data centers all around the world.

Time moved on and so did I. I found myself working for Siemens, the big German telecommunications company. They were making phone switches and selling them to the seven U.S. phone companies. The problem was that the switches were too complicated. Customers couldn't tell the difference between one complicated phone switch from another complicated phone switch. Once again I found myself working with customers to create solutions that would allow them to add complicated equipment to their network while still being able to remotely monitor and control it.

I've spent over 25 years working as a data center product manager for both big companies and startups. This has given me an opportunity to create many, many PDU solutions for customers.

I now live in Tampa Florida where I spend my time managing my consulting business, Blue Elephant Consulting, teaching college courses at the University of South Florida, and traveling to work with companies like yours to share the knowledge that I have about how to create power distribution unit solutions that work with modern data centers.

I'm always available to answer questions and I can be reached at:

Dr. Jim Anderson
Blue Elephant Consulting
Email: jim@BlueElephantConsulting.com
Facebook: http://goo.gl/1TVoK
Web: http://www.BlueElephantConsulting.com/

"Unforgettable communication skills that will set your ideas free..."

Chapter 1

Power Distribution Units (PDU): What Are They?

Power Distribution Units (PDU): What Are They?

If your career has anything to do with a data center, you know one of those places where "cloud computing" lives, then you NEED to know what a Power Distribution Unit (PDU) is. With the answer to the question "what is a PDU?" you'll be one step closer to fully understanding how a data center operates – and just what might go wrong if you're not careful!

What Is A PDU?

In a data center, metal monsters called "racks" are used to house computer servers in a vertical stacking arrangement. You could stack up to 42 servers in a single rack if you had to. However, that's when you start to run into real problems: how are you going to provide power to all of those computers? The solution to that problem turns out to be what is called a power distribution unit or "a rack PDU".

The 1st Generation Of PDUs

The field of PDUs is a fast growing and constantly changing field. As the demands of the computer servers in the data centers keep changing, the manufactures of PDUs have been racing to keep up. There have been four generations of rack PDUs so far.

In the first generation of PDUs, called "unintelligent PDUs", a PDU was very similar to the power strips that you and I use in our homes. However, these PDUs were mounted horizontally inside of a rack. Each rack PDU provided up to 8 power outlets and the problem of powering servers was solved – or was it?

The horizontal rack PDUs suffered from two critical flaws: they took up room in the rack that could be better used for adding more servers and they just didn't provide enough outlets. The PDU vendors took a look at the rack environment and made an interesting discovery. There was plenty of room in the back of the rack if they changed how rack PDUs were positioned.

They were switched from horizontal to vertical, and were attached to the sides of the rack. This also provided the vendors with more room which allowed them to grow the size of the rack PDUs to now each contain between 16 and 48 outlets. Because everyone realized how critical the rack PDUs had become to the correct operation of the rack, two rack PDUs are now added to each rack in order to provide redundancy by providing a primary and a secondary rack PDU.

The 2nd Generation Of PDUs

Innovation is a strange beast, it can show up in the most unexpected places. In the case of PDUs, once the maximum number of outlets that they could offer had been reached, vendors who were competing with each other to offer the best PDU knew that they had to make their PDUs do something besides just deliver electricity. This resulted in two key features being added in order to create the second generation of intelligent rack PDUs: switching and metering.

A rack PDU with switching functionality allowed a remote user to turn a given socket on the PDU either on or off. This feature is useful for remotely rebooting a server who's software has malfunctioned, or for deactivating unused sockets so that the night cleaning crew doesn't plug in a vacuum cleaner to your PDU and cause your entire rack power system to overload and shut down.

A 2nd generation rack PDU provided metering for the entire PDU which meant that customers now had a means of getting basic overload protection (to monitor circuits) and rough capacity estimating.

Chapter 2

Moving From The 3rd To The 4th Generation Of PDUs

Chapter 2

Moving From The 3rd To The 4th Generation Of PDUs

Moving From The 3rd To The 4th Generation Of PDUs

Power distribution units (PDUs) have come a long way in just a few years. From their humble beginnings as first generation unintelligent electrical distribution systems that simply provided an electrical outlet for a server, they've evolved into second generation intelligent rack PDUs that now support switched service and energy metering on a per PDU basis. No longer do people ask "What are PDUs", instead they are now asking "Which PDU is right for my data center?"

The 3rd Generation Of PDUs

For a while first generation rack PDUs met most customers' data center needs; however, over time customers started asking for more. Vendors delivered what customers were asking for when they created 2nd generation PDUs that supported both switching and metering functionality.

You'd might have thought that the second generation rack PDUs were the last step, that there was nothing else that vendors could do to extend the functionality of something as simple as a PDU. Well guess what, you'd be wrong. The third generation of PDU evolution happened next.

Energy metering was enhanced from just monitoring the whole PDU to now providing metering information on an individual socket level. This type of information allowed data center operators to manage their own energy usage and provided them with a way to charge co-lo customers for the energy that their racks were using.

Adding Environmental Sensors To PDUs

Rack environmental sensors were added to second generation rack PDUs. This change makes sense: the PDUs were already communicating with remote users and systems in order to support their switching and metering functions, reporting on and controlling local sensors was the next logical step.

What happened here is that the humble PDU was transformed into a rack environment monitoring solution. A single rack PDU could now report on multiple rack environmental variables including temperature, humidity, if a rack door had been opened, if there were fluids on the floor, and if any smoke was present in the rack environment.

The 4th Generation Of PDUs

Now the next generation of PDUS, the 4th generation, has arrived. Many different companies are currently producing 4th generation rack PDUs. These PDUs are distinguished by the shift in their focus from just providing rack environmental data to now allowing data center operators to take control of their rack environment. This can be done in a number of different ways.

Ease of use was a key driver for vendors when they were creating the 4th generation rack PDUs. In order to support data center hosting of co-lo customers, higher accuracy ("billing grade") metering for chargeback models has been incorporated into these rack PDUs. Additionally, advanced efficiency metrics are now also included so that a complete picture of energy usage on both a PDU and a per socket basis can be delivered by the rack PDU to upstream software monitoring systems.

4th generation rack PDUs now open the door for data center owners / operators to finally be able to predict the future. Using sophisticated software, the data streams that the rack PDUs are reporting about device energy usage and the rack's environmental status can be analyzed and for the first time the early indications of equipment failure can be detected BEFORE a failure occurs.

No, this is not an easy thing to do; however, the ability to forecast and prevent data center outages is an invaluable feature that only 4th generation rack PDUs will be able to provide.

Chapter 3

What's The Difference Between A Power Distribution Unit And A Boeing 787?

What's The Difference Between A Power Distribution Unit And A Boeing 787?

Power distribution units (PDUs) tend to sit quietly in data centers providing power to racks of computer servers and connecting to the data center's electrical power supply system. Boeing's 787 is their newest aircraft which has been created using space-age composite materials and has the ability to fly farther, faster, and at a lower cost than any other aircraft that has ever been created. You wouldn't think that these two things would have much in common would you? That's where you'd be wrong...

The Problem With Planes That Use Batteries

The Boeing 787 has run into some problems with its design. What kind of problems you ask? Electrical problems! The plane uses lithium-ion batteries instead of older lead-acid batteries because the lithium-ion batteries hold a much larger electrical charge and they weigh less than the older style of battery. However, something has gone very, very wrong with the batteries that Boeing has put on their 787s.

Boeing knew that they had an electrical problem when a battery burst into flames on Boeing 787 that was sitting on a runway in Boston. This problem with an airplane matters to those of us who work in data centers is that this electrical event didn't just suddenly happen – it could have been predicted.

How Are PDUs Like An Airplane?

That's right – even in our data centers, our servers don't just fail. Instead, they often send up warning signals long before a failure occurs. In the case of the Boeing 787s, the jet that eventually had the battery fire experienced dramatic power fluctuations and other failures that its designers had thought that could never happen. Does any of this sound familiar to you?

When it comes to providing power to servers in a data center, the last line of defense that you have against bad power is your PDUs. If you have deployed the so-called "dumb" PDUs, you'll never know if you are starting to have a problem. However, if you've invested in 4th generation "smart" PDUs then you'll have the ability to detect changes in your electrical distribution system long before they can cause problems for your servers.

Just how much do you have invested in you data center's power infrastructure? A lot. Don't throw it all away and allow your precious servers to be powered by cheap and faulty PDUs. Take the time to study what options you have when it comes to selecting the right PDU for your servers.

A number of today's PDU vendors can provide you with PDUs that have a low-profile design, are rated for rock-solid performance even at high data center temperatures, and come with swappable components. By taking the time to choose the right PDU, you can make sure that you don't run into the same problems that Boeing has run into with their 787s!

Chapter 4

Unexpected Uses For Power Distribution Units (PDUs)

Unexpected Uses For Power Distribution Units (PDUs)

Power distribution units (PDUs) have been built with one job in mind: providing safe, reliable, power for servers that are housed in a data center. PDU vendors struggle to keep pace with all of the rapid changes that are sweeping through the PDU market. More often than once, how customer have decided to use their PDUs has caught a PDU vendor by surprise.

You'd think that since PDU vendors spend their days doing nothing but designing, building, investigating, and experimenting with PDUs they'd know it all. You'd think that they would have thought of every possible way that their customers could use their PDUs. If you did, you'd be wrong. Not a week goes by that a PDU vendor doesn't get a call from a customer thanking them for their PDUs and telling them about a novel way that they are using them.

Today's modern PDUs have been designed to be used in the harsh environment of a modern data center. When a customer buy a PDU from a PDU vendor, that's where they expect them to end up. However, more and more they're finding that their customers are purchasing our PDUs to use in their testing labs.

The ability to deliver 16A, 30A, or even 32A to a testing work bench is turning out to be invaluable. Additionally, the vendor's PDU's built-in metering functionality that allows the energy usage to be monitored down to the outlet level allows a technician to do away with other expensive current and voltage monitoring gear and just use the PDU's functionality. This is only possible because the vendor's units are provide billing grade metering resolution to +/- 1%

We're all familiar with what a data center looks like, right? We can picture the rows and rows of neatly stacked racks and we may even be able to picture the backs of those racks that will have two PDUs per rack hung there in order to provide clean, reliable power to all of the servers and associated networking gear. However, some customers have created a brand new environment for the vendor's PDUs: the assembly line.

A European car manufacturer recently informed me that they are using a vendor's PDUs to provide power to the various robots and monitoring systems that they have working on their automobile assembly line. It makes sense after all: assembly lines can stretch on for literally miles and if an electrical device starts to act up, cycling power is a quick and easy fix. Using the vendor's PDU's switching functionality the auto manufacture can easily allow authorized staff to cycle power remotely, get the device back up and running all without having to shut the assembly line down or walk out to the dangerous, noisy position on the line where the fault has occurred.

One customer called me up the other day just to thank me for helping him to finally be able to create a business case that he'd be trying to get approved for years. Now I'm used to having customers plug state-of-the-art servers and network gear into a 4th Generation PDUs. However, this customer had purchased an inline energy meters and connected to one of their old computer room air conditioning units (CRAC).

This antique has been using way too much electricity for years, but this customer could never quantify just how much it was using. With the use of the inline energy meter, he was able to use the metering functionality and was finally able to come up with some hard numbers for the total cost of NOT replacing the unit. Needless to say, he got his money for the CRAC unit upgrade!

I'm sure that all PDU vendors probably have a lot of other customers out there that are using PDUs in ways that we have never even dreamed of. They have been designed to provide clean, reliable power with a wealth of 4th Generation features and functionality. Customers keep showing that once they have this powerful tool in their hands, there is no limit to what problems they can solve with it!

Chapter 5

The Limitations Of Using Thermal Fuses In Data Centers

The Limitations Of Using Thermal Fuses In Data Centers

How much does a modern data center cost? Millions? Hundreds of millions? The total cost of building a data center is increasing every day. Why do these buildings cost so much?

The answer is simple: the job that they do is hard to do perfectly. A modern data center is designed to provide a secure, reliable home to hundreds (or even thousands) of servers. Servers that run mission critical software for companies all over the world. One part of a data center's job is to provide reliable, clean, power to each of the servers in the data center..

Here in the 21st century, that part of the job would be relatively simple, right? In our homes, when we flip switches things happen: lights turn on, the computer powers up, or the TV flickers on. However, think about all of the times that you've lost power or how often the lights flicker. A data center is designed to prevent these types of events.

When it comes to the job of providing power to servers, data center designers have a primary task to accomplish. This task is to create an electrical distribution system that will provide reliable power and avoid unsafe operating conditions. But doing this is more difficult than you might imagine.

How Are Servers Kept On All the Time?

To ensure that servers always have power, data center designers go to great lengths. They often build two completely separate and redundant electrical power distribution systems along with multiple types of power backup solutions. These expensive and complex solutions ensure that if power to the data center is ever lost, backup systems can quickly provide the needed energy. Additionally, if there is ever a failure of one of the redundant power systems, the secondary system can provide the required electricity until the failed system is repaired.

What makes all of the expensive design so fascinating is that it all comes down to a single component to ensure that all of the servers continue to receive the energy required in order to stay powered up: the rack power distribution unit (rack PDU). The rack PDU receives electricity from the data center's redundant power delivery systems and it is responsible for delivering that energy to the individual servers and IT equipment. If the rack PDU fails, then the servers will fail.

The rack PDU is a data center operator's last line of defense against accidental circuit overloads and harmful faults. In many countries, the rack PDU includes design features that are required by electric code and mandatory industry standards requiring protection against these events. As such, rack PDU vendors incorporate solutions to for these occurrences.

The Problem with Fuses in a Data Center

How does a PDU keep the data center servers safe from dangerous overcurrent and fault conditions? There are many ways for a PDU to do this, but the least expensive method (in terms of cost to PDU vendors) is by the use of thermal fuses.

Fuses are a special type of resistor that exists for one purpose: to fail when exposed to electrical currents beyond the designed capacity. A fuse works by allowing the incoming current to flow over a piece of metal designed to melt when the current exceeds the rated limit. When an overcurrent condition occurs, the metal melts, the circuit is broken, and the electrical flow is interrupted.

The servers will lose power; however, if the fuse melts quickly enough the servers will not be damaged or destroyed. Because the fuse is designed to melt as a function of temperature, the use of fuses in thermally hot environments requires a "derating" of the current carrying capacity. In a data center, this means that a fuse rated for 16A or 20A might melt (or fail) at electrical currents lower than the designed because of the hot data center environment that they are being used in. Failure to account for this derating results in a tripping of the fuse during normally safe operation.

Fuses have other negative attributes when they are used in a data center. Sure, a fuse can step in and save the servers in an overcurrent event, however, it's what you have to do after such an event that makes fuses no longer an acceptable solution for data center application.

Once a fuse has blown, it must be replaced. This replacement is dangerous for the user. As a result, the entire rack PDU must be powered down. Often this type of replacement must be performed by a licensed electrician. And the electrician must have the correct fuses on hand to replace the blown fuse.

Considering that if a current overload condition occurs, you'll probably have fuses in all of the PDUs that are connected to that power source blow, you may be looking at an expensive and time consuming repair job. As long as those blown fuses are still installed in PDUs, all of the servers are going to be running on a single backup power source after the failure occurs. If a fault occurs to that backup power source, then all of the severs will be lost. While fuses are inexpensive, recovering from a blown fuse can be devastating in terms of cost and downtime in the data center environment.

Chapter 6

Thermal Breakers Have Real World Limits In A Data Center

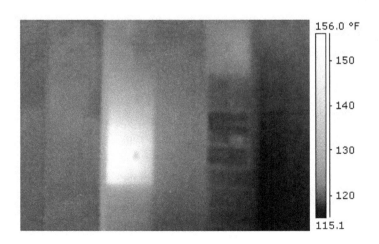

Thermal Breakers Have Real World Limits In A Data Center

In a modern data center to ensure that servers always have power, data center designers go to great lengths. They often build two completely separate and redundant electrical power distribution systems along with multiple types of power backup solutions.

These expensive and complex solutions ensure that if power to the data center is ever lost, backup systems can quickly provide the needed energy. Additionally, if there is ever a failure of one of the redundant power systems, the secondary system can provide the required electricity until the failed system is repaired.

What makes all of the expensive design so fascinating is that it all comes down to a single component to ensure that all of the servers continue to receive the energy required in order to stay powered up: the rack power distribution unit (rack PDU).

What are PDUs you ask? The rack PDU receives electricity from the data center's redundant power delivery systems and it is responsible for delivering that energy to the individual servers and IT equipment. If the rack PDU fails, then the servers will fail.

The rack PDU is a data center operator's last line of defense against accidental circuit overloads and harmful faults. In many countries, the rack PDU includes design features that are required by electric code and mandatory industry standards requiring protection against these events. As such, rack PDU vendors incorporate solutions to for these occurrences.

Circuit Breakers and PDUs: A Match Made In Heaven

Circuit breakers detect overcurrent (or fault) situations and break the electrical circuit providing power. How they do this and how well they do it is what distinguishes one PDU from another.

In a circuit breaker, an internal pilot device senses a fault current and trips the device. When a circuit overload condition occurs, contacts in the circuit breaker have to open to interrupt the circuit. To separate the metal contacts mechanically, stored energy within the breaker opens the circuit.

All PDU Circuit Breakers Are Not Created the Same

There are different types of circuit breakers available. Different types of circuit breakers have different costs and physical size. When vendors build rack PDUs, they have to make a cost / benefit decision about which circuit breaker they will use. The type of circuit breaker has a significant impact on how well servers are protected against fault conditions and accidental tripping.

Two different types of circuit breakers are often used in PDUs, and although these two different types of circuit breakers perform the same job, they do it differently based on performance characteristics

1. Thermal-based circuit breakers

2. Hydraulic-magnetic (hy-mag) circuit breakers

Thermal-based circuit breakers are also known as thermal circuit breakers or thermal-magnetic circuit breakers. These thermal-based circuit breakers are made using a bi-metallic strip. This strip has two different pieces of metal welded together, each meant to expand when in contact with the heat of an electric current. With two different kinds of metal, the expansion rate for each is different. The thermal based circuit breaker depends on the heat generated by the passing electrical current; the greater the heat, the more severely the metal strip bends.

When there is an electric overload, the heat generated bends the strip enough to pull the circuit level to the off position, protecting the wiring from damage. When a thermal circuit breaker is reset, it is likely to trip again if the overload condition still exists.

The problem with using a thermal circuit breaker in a PDU is that they are susceptible to unintended tripping when used in high temperature environments like a data center. Because the PDU is contained in a rack and is exposed to high temperatures, the PDU's thermal circuit breaker can accidentally trip and lose power. The trip setting of a typical thermal circuit breaker changes due to ambient temperature; for many rack PDUs, the trip setting can vary by more than 15%.

Another challenge when using a thermal circuit breaker is the tripping temperature changes by more than 15% over the rack PDU's operating temperature specification! Thermal circuit breaker vendors recommend to keep a PDU's load current at 80% or less of the rated current to account for the variation in temperature that the external rack temperature can cause a trip. This restricts total power output per rack, and results in unplanned downtime conditions.

An alternative type of circuit breaker used in a PDU is the type used by many PDU vendors: the hydraulic-magnetic, or hy-mag, circuit breaker. The hy-mag breaker is independent of temperature as a tripping mechanism Hy-mag breaker's tripping mechanism does not use thermal elements (bimetal) and is not affected by ambient rack temperature. Sure hy-mag breakers cost the vendor a bit more; however, when it comes to protecting all of the valuable servers that you have in your racks, it's well worth it.

Chapter 7

Why Buying Cheap PDUs Are Never A Good Idea

Why Buying Cheap PDUs Are Never A Good Idea

I like a bargain, you like a bargain, we all like bargains. However, that old phrase "you get what you pay for" has never been more true than when it comes to buying power distribution units (PDUs) for your data center. There are countless vendors out there who all make a dizzying array of products and at times it can seem to be a very difficult task to choose between them. Why not just pick the cheapest one – I mean after all, we're just talking about power strips, right?

If It Looks Too Good To Be True...

One of the advantages of working with data center owners and operators is that I get a chance to talk with EVERYONE in the business. I've recently spent time in discussions with several data center teams who are located in the Baltic region. This is one of the, pardon the phrase, hottest places to build a new data center, Facebook is current building their new data center in Lulea, Sweden and a lot of other firms are following them. The low cost of energy and the ready availability of cooling makes this part of the world a great place to have a data center.

What this means for me is that this is a highly competitive market for data center equipment vendors and that means that data center operators have a large number of choices when it comes to selecting the PDUs that they'll use. Lately, a number of low-cost Asian manufactures have shown up in the market with some incredible offers.

The products that are in their catalog look great. They appear to have almost every feature that you could want in a modern 4th generation PDU. If you see the units at a trade show, they appear to be solidly built. Finally, the prices that they are charging are amazingly low – it's almost like they are giving them away! Maybe data center staff should be getting a little nervous at this point in time, but a number that I've talked with told me that at those low prices, their minds were made up on the spot. What could possibly go wrong?

Under The Hood Of A PDU

The answer to that question is a lot. I've taken the time to buying some of these Asian PDUs and then voiding the warranty by immediately opening them up to see what they look like on the inside. I know why these low-cost PDUs are priced so low – a lot of corners have been cut in the design and manufacturing of these units. However, most customers don't open their low-cost PDUs up so they have to find out the hard way.

My Scandinavian colleagues who had selected the low-cost Asian PDUs were excited to get the first batch. Once they arrived, they immediately took them into their lab for a complete check out. What they found disappointed them. The impact of selecting a low-cost PDU became apparent very quickly: the use of cheap fuses coupled with a poorly engineered design resulted in a PDU that provided unstable switching. Sometimes it switched, sometimes it did not.

Their second discovery also clearly showed the reason that they should not have selected a cheap PDU. Although the catalog had listed an impressive number of features for the PDU, testing revealed that some of the features were only partially implemented and others were missing all together.

Final Chapter

Saving money is something that we all want to do because we don't have unlimited budgets and we would like to be able to spend our limited funds wisely. When we are presented with the opportunity to buy cheap PDUs, we need to stop for a moment and consider what we are being presented with.

A PDU represents your last line of defense before the data center's electrical power reaches your servers. Those servers are the lifeblood of your business. They must continue to receive clean, reliable power at all times.

Saving a little bit of money on a component of your electrical distribution system that you've already potentially spent a great deal on seems like a poor decision. Take the time to learn what has to go into a PDU in order to create a design that won't let you down and who's long-term reliable operation will free you up to worry about all of the other things that go on in a modern data center on a daily basis. Remember, you get what you pay for!

Chapter 8

Why Data Center Operators Are Switching To Using Hy-Mag

Why Data Center Operators Are Switching To Using Hy-Mag

In a modern data center to ensure that servers always have power, data center designers go to great lengths. They often build two completely separate and redundant electrical power distribution systems along with multiple types of power backup solutions.

These expensive and complex solutions ensure that if power to the data center is ever lost, backup systems can quickly provide the needed energy. Additionally, if there is ever a failure of one of the redundant power systems, the secondary system can provide the required electricity until the failed system is repaired.

What makes all of the expensive design so fascinating is that it all comes down to a single component to ensure that all of the servers continue to receive the energy required in order to stay powered up: the rack power distribution unit (rack PDU).

What are PDUs you ask? The rack PDU receives electricity from the data center's redundant power delivery systems and it is responsible for delivering that energy to the individual servers and IT equipment. If the rack PDU fails, then the servers will fail.

The rack PDU is a data center operator's last line of defense against accidental circuit overloads and harmful faults. In many countries, the rack PDU includes design features that are required by electric code and mandatory industry standards requiring protection against these events. As such, rack PDU vendors incorporate solutions to for these occurrences.

The rack PDU is a data center operator's last line of defense against accidental circuit overloads and harmful faults. In many countries, the rack PDU includes design features that are required by electric code and mandatory industry standards requiring protection against these events. As such, rack PDU vendors incorporate solutions to for these occurrences.

In a circuit breaker, an internal pilot device senses a fault current and trips the device. When a circuit overload condition occurs, contacts in the circuit breaker have to open to interrupt the circuit. To separate the metal contacts mechanically, stored energy within the breaker opens the circuit.

All PDU Circuit Breakers Are Not Created the Same

There are different types of circuit breakers available. Different types of circuit breakers have different costs and physical size. When vendors build rack PDUs, they have to make a cost / benefit decision about which circuit breaker they will use. The type of circuit breaker has a significant impact on how well servers are protected against fault conditions and accidental tripping.

Two different types of circuit breakers are often used in PDUs, and although these two different types of circuit breakers perform the same job, they do it differently based on performance characteristics

- Thermal-based circuit breakers
- Hydraulic-magnetic (hy-mag) circuit breakers

What Are Hydraulic-Magnetic Circuit Breakers?

Many PDU vendors use the hydraulic-magnetic, or hy-mag, circuit breaker in our PDUs. The hy-mag breaker is independent of temperature as a tripping mechanism Hy-mag breaker's tripping mechanism does not use thermal elements (bimetal) and is not affected by ambient rack temperature.

Rather, the current load is connected through a solenoid coil. At currents above the circuit breaker rating, the coil generates magnetic flux necessary to force a spring mechanism to open the electrical circuit and prevent current flow through the breaker. What this means is that the tripping current is related to the amount of current only; the hy-mag breaker will keep consistent tripping characteristics across the entire range of data center ambient temperatures.

When a circuit breaker trips, the data center operator wants the affected servers powered up as quickly as possible. This is where another big difference between fuses and circuit breakers, and further between thermal and hydraulic-magnetic circuit breakers becomes clear.

When a circuit breaker trips or fuse blows, users should explore why the event occurred and take action to prevent reoccurrence. However, in the case of a fuse: the entire rack PDU must be powered down and specially trained personnel must replace the blown fuse.

In the case of the resettable circuit breaker: the circuit failure is often isolated to just one portion of the rack PDU output. Users can independently eliminate the fault condition and reset the circuit breaker without powering down the remainder of the rack PDU. Further, circuit breakers don't require specially trained personnel to reset the device after failure.

When a hydraulic-magnetic circuit breaker is tripped, it provides the ability to be instantaneously reset once you've corrected the cause of the circuit failure. This is not the case with thermal circuit breakers.

With thermal circuit breakers, the once the bimetal has been bent due to the tripping event, it does not immediately return to its original position. Instead, this circuit breaker remains tripped until the bimetal is cooled. The time from the circuit breaker tripping until it can be reset is called the reset time.

Reset time can vary between 3–20 minutes depending on the breaker. Sure hy-mag breakers cost the vendor a bit more; however, when it comes to protecting all of the valuable servers that you have in your racks, it's well worth it.

Chapter 9

Data Center Operator Lessons From The World Of Formula 1 Auto Racing

Data Center Operator Lessons From The World Of Formula 1 Auto Racing

As we all grow up, we seem to pick one sport that we like above all others. For many of us this may be football because we played it as children, or depending on where you grew up it might be baseball or cricket. However, in my case for some strange and unusual reason the sport that I adopted was Formula 1 racing.

What You Need To Know About Formula 1 Racing

So what is this sport called Formula 1? Formula 1 is the top-of-the-top when it comes to racing. The cars are single-seaters that race in a series of races called Grand Prix which are hosted at glamorous spots all over the world. Because the sport is so expensive, drivers have to belong to well-funded teams. Each year there are two prizes given out: one for the best driver and one for the best team.

The reason that I love watching Formula 1 racing so much is that it is very FAST. The cars reach speeds upwards of 350 km/h (220 mph). Formula 1 cars are the most engineered cars in the world: the challenge is to find out how to get the most out of an engine that is limited to 18,000 RPM, along with optimizing its aerodynamics and tires. Every team starts with the same rules, but it's how they design a car to those rules that makes the sport so facilitating.

What Does Formula 1 Have To With Running A Data Center?

Along about now you might be asking yourself just exactly what Formula 1 racing has to do with the business of running a data center? It turns out that there are a lot of similarities. The one that I wanted to focus on right now is the issues of down time and why it's so bad.

When you watch a Formula 1 race, one of the most interesting parts is how each of the teams handles their pit stops. The cars decelerate from their high speeds and pull into pit lane. They find where their team is setup and they come to a halt. Now the clock starts ticking. The pit crew has a list of different tasks that they need to complete as quickly as possible. Filling the gas tank, changing one or more tires, fixing the suspension, replacing faulty electronics, etc. It has often been said that a Formula 1 race is lost not on the track, but in the pits.

Data center operators face the same challenges. When a device that they use to manage their data center fails, all of a sudden they are blind. They no longer have access to the information that that device had been providing them with and they need to get it fixed. There's no pit stop in a data center, but there is a clock that starts ticking when vital data center operational information has been lost and has to be restored.

PDUs In The Pit Lane

One of the most important devices, right after servers, that are deployed in a data center are the power distribution units (PDUs). These are the devices that both provide power to servers and thanks to the sensors that can be plugged into them enable an operator to monitor the status of their very expensive racks. When a PDU fails, the operator no longer knows what's happening in that rack and this problem needs to be fixed as quickly as possible.

The good news about a PDU failure is that more often than not, the devices that are plugged in to the PDU will still be getting the electrical energy that they need in order to continue to operate. However, that PDU will more than likely have experienced a failure of its network control card and so it will no longer be able to talk to the data center operator or be configured by technical staff. Something has got to be changed.

For the first three generations of PDUs, this meant that the entire PDU had to be removed from the rack and replaced with a new PDU. This was a major undertaking.

41

The data center operator had to get permission from each of the owners of the servers that were plugged into the PDU in order to turn their server off while the PDU was replaced. In talking with our customers, Industry studies have shown that if you include all of the paperwork that getting these permissions required, a project like this could take upwards of 80 staff hours. Please note that this is for the failure of a single PDU – failure of multiple PDUs would take much, much longer to repair.

The understanding of just how important minimizing the time that data center operators spend in the pit lane drove the development of 4th generator of PDUs. Vendors understood the importance of minimizing the amount of time that a PDU is "down". A vendor's high-quality construction techniques should, under normal circumstances, ensure that there are no product failures.

However, in the event that a network control card was to fail, a data center's pit crew could quickly fix the problem. Many modern PDUs come with a swappable control card. This means that if one was to fail, all that a technician would have to do to fix it would be to remove two screws, unplug the failed card, plug a new one in and tighten two screws. Total time involved: 2 minutes. Number of servers turned off: 0. Guess who's going to win this race?

Chapter 10

Why Dumb PDUs Are Still Popular In Data Centers!

Why Dumb PDUs Are Still Popular In Data Centers

In my job, I get a chance to sit down and have very frank discussions with different data center owners and operators all around the world every day. I'm always asking them questions about how they want to improve their business and what they believe their biggest challenges are – you know, the normal sort of questions that vendors always ask customers. However, some of the answers that I've been getting lately have just been amazing!

What Is A "Dumb PDU"?

I live in the world of data center power – specifically getting power to all of those servers that live in all of those racks. This means that I'm always talking with my customers about how they can use less electricity and how they can get that electricity to their servers more reliably at a lower total cost. This means that the discussion is always eventually going to come around to talking about power distribution units (PDUs).

The world of PDUs is currently divided up into two separate groups. There is the classic "dumb PDU" and the more modern "intelligent PDU". The dumb PDUs are exactly what you'd think that they are – dumb. These PDUs exist to do one thing and one thing only – provide power to whatever device that is plugged into to them. They don't track or monitor anything and they have no ability to be networked. They just sit quietly in the corner and provide power. End of story.

Intelligent PDUs on the other hand, provide a great deal of functionality above and beyond just providing power to plugged in devices. Intelligent PDUs can monitor how much energy the PDU or even individual outlets are using, they can turn outlets on and off, support multiple sensors, and, of course, they can be networked in order to both provide information and accept control commands.

If an intelligent PDU does so much more than a dumb PDU, who wouldn't want to buy / upgrade to one of these? Well, some data center owners / operators are very much driven by their bottom line (does this sound like anyone that you know?) and when it comes time to expand or upgrade their data center, they take a look at the price of everything. As you might well expect, intelligent PDUs cost more than dumb PDUs. Or do they?

I was talking with a data center owner the other day and, as always, the conversation got around to PDUs. He informed me that he appreciated me telling him all about the 4th Generation PDUs but he was going to stick with his dumb PDUs because that was all that he felt that he needed. Hmm, sure looked like we needed to do some more talking.

I asked him a simple question: how do your customers know if their server has gone down? He replied that they tried to access it, were not able to, then they picked up the phone and called him. I asked him what happened next. He told me that he would then send one of his workers down to the data center floor, over the rack that contained the offending server, and they would then check the server's status lights.

If it had failed or locked up, they would then cycle power on it. I asked if one of his workers had ever cycled power on the wrong server. He sheepishly admitted that yes, this had happened a couple of times. I then asked him roughly how long it took from phone call until the customer's server was back up and running. He told me that he thought that it took about an hour on average.

An hour of down time for a customer? Ouch. Now I know that every customer is not like Amazon, but they've reported that a minute of downtime costs them US$100,000. How much does an hour cost your customers? The reason that a down server can take this data center owner so long to get back up is because he's blind when it comes to what is going on in his rack. He's got no way to tell what's running and what's fallen over.

Let's take a look at the same scenario if he'd been willing to make the investment in an intelligent PDU. First off, he wouldn't need to the customer to call him to tell him that his server had died – the PDU would report that the power usage by the server had dropped to zero.

An alarm would have been automatically generated for the data center owner. Next, using the PDU's automatic switching functionality, the socket that that PDU was plugged into could have been cycled off / on. The server would have then automatically rebooted. Total downtime would have been roughly 2 minutes and the customer may have never even known that there was a problem.

Needless to say, this is the very discussion that I had with my customer and in the end he saw the error of his way. Yes, he could save some upfront money by purchasing a dumb PDU, but it was going to cost him a lot more in the long run. Additionally, with the intelligent PDUs he would now have a competitive feature that would allow him to attract more customers than his competition.

Chapter 11

One Size Does NOT Fit All:
The Story of Goldilocks
and the Three PDUs

One Size Does NOT Fit All: The Story of Goldilocks and the Three PDUs

I'm pretty sure that we can all remember the story of Goldilocks and the three bears from our childhood. A key part of that story is that Goldilocks is always struggling to find the right solution no matter if it involves bowls of porridge or comfortable beds.

When you either own or operate a data center, just like Goldilocks your life is constantly filled with having to make decisions. If only there was some way to make your life simpler (before the bears come home!) The reason that you are called on to make so many decisions is that for every problem that you face, there are multiple vendors and multiple product configurations that might be able to solve your problem.

I'm sorry that I can't make this problem go away for you, but I just might be able to share a story with you about how one data center owner went about making some important decisions that could help you to more easily make your own set of decisions quicker and better...

The Problem With Growth

A company that I was working with lately had a problem that we all probably wish that we had. They were experiencing unprecedented growth in all three of their lines of businesses and it had become time to play the role of Goldilocks and make some difficult decisions. This company is an international IT services company that has two main branches that provide IT services: we'll call them Branch 1 and Branch 2.

The Branch 1 division of the company is an IT service provider who both owns and operates their own data centers. They specialize in offering cloud computing infrastructures to their customers. Since 2009 they have been experiencing rapid growth every year. Starting in 2007 Branch 1 had envisioned the idea of a virtual data center and had moved forward and started to build their own cloud computing environment. This is a competitive marketplace in which they find themselves competing with the likes of Google, Amazon, and Microsoft.

The Branch 2 division of the company is a systems integrator that helps to provide its customers with complex IT solutions. The solutions that Branch 2 designs for its customers include cloud based solutions, consulting services, and security services.

Both of these divisions of were facing the same set of challenges that rapid growth had forced upon them: they needed to expand their data centers, they needed to create reliable power infrastructures, and they had to spend their limited budgets wisely if they wanted to keep on growing. Does any of this sound familiar to you? Their engineers and data center planners knew that they were facing a very large challenge.

Working together, the Branch 1 and Branch 2 planners first decided to evaluate their power needs in order to make sure that any solutions that they designed would be sure to provide them with all of the functionality that they were going to need for both today and tomorrow.

As the engineers held planning discussions, one thing quickly became clear to all involved. The company didn't just have one set of needs that had to be met; rather they had three distinct sets of requirements that they were going to have to find a way to solve.

First, they were going to have to continue to build out their cloud infrastructure in order to meet the needs of their customers who had committed to moving their IT infrastructure to the cloud. Next, their profitable hosting business was going to continue to expand for the foreseeable future and so they were going to need a great deal more floor space in order to support both existing customers who wanted to expand as well as new customers who were looking for a high-quality hosting environment. Finally, the traditional data center services that both divisions of the company offered were going to continue to expand also.

Growth is always a good thing, but the company was facing a huge challenge in trying to create a power design that would support the three different ways that their company was growing.

Realizing that they probably were not going to be able to find a single power solution that would meet the needs of all three of their different IT data center environments, the engineering design teams started to build separate requirements lists for each of the environments.

It was about at this time that the company's executives traveled to the annual CeBIT IT trade show that was being held in Hannover, Germany. It was an effort to take the time off to attend this show and they went with no clear goal in mind; however, they knew that this was the show where all of the latest technology would be on display and perhaps they would discover a vendor who might be able to help them create power designs that would work in all three of their IT data center environments.

That year's CeBIT happened to be the year that I had attended the show in order to research the rack power distribution unit (PDU) manufacturers. Because the world is a small place and because when it comes to data centers everyone knows everyone else, the company's teams and I ended up meeting each other and exchanging business cards.

The company's team explained the power challenges that they were facing and then I proposed taking the time for both teams to sit down and explore what a solution might look like. The company team agreed and a date was set.

The first challenge that the two teams tacked was the Branch 1 division's need to expand their cloud computing facilities. The engineering teams had identified that in the new facility that they were going to be building, they wanted to have more control over what was happening at the rack level.

Specifically, what they were looking for was a way to determine how much electrical energy each server that was part of the cloud was currently using. There were a number of different ways to provide this information; however, many of them required additional equipment and the further away from the rack that they were, the less accurate the energy usage numbers that they would be reporting would be.

I proposed that Branch 1 consider installing a 4th generation PDU for use in their new Cloud Data Center space. This PDU had been designed to provide its user with energy usage metering on a per outlet basis.

The Branch 1 engineers would be able to get real-time 24x7x365 information in the form of V, A, VA, W, kWh, and pf. This would finally provide Branch 1 with the ability to determine server energy usage down to the +/- 1% level. Ultimately, using this information Branch 1 engineers would be able to monitor their overall energy usage and create solid business cases to justify the upgrading of specific servers with more energy efficient models.

The next challenge that was tackled was the Branch 1 hosting solution. This posed a unique set of challenges for the Branch 1 engineers. For their hosted customers they needed to know how much energy was being used at a per-outlet level as well as having the ability to turn off power on a per outlet level. Upon hearing these unique requirements, I suggested that the Branch 1 engineers take a look at a 4th generation PDU that was at the top of the line in terms of the functionality. Metering that was accurate to +/- 1% was provided down to the outlet level along with per outlet switching functionality. It appeared as though a single PDU could meet all of Branch 1's hosting rack needs.

Finally, the conversation got around to Branch 2's Data Center expansion plans. For this IT environment, they were looking for a fairly simple solution. They needed an economical solution that would allow them to know how much electrical energy was being used by a rack in their data center.

They didn't need to know energy usage down to the server level, just to the rack level. I suggested that a simpler PDU which provided per PDU metering might be what the Branch 2 team was looking for.

This Goldilocks story had a happy ending – the customer found exactly what they were looking for in the end. However, the key thing to realize here is that the answer that they needed was not provided by a single product. Instead, it took different products with different features to meet all of their growth needs. Next time you find yourself playing the role of Goldilocks, be sure to check out all of the bowls of porridge and all of beds in order to make sure that you've found the right solution for your data center.

Chapter 12

Data Center Risk: What Beginning Drivers And Data Center Operators Have In Common

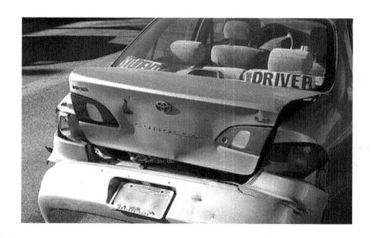

Data Center Risk: What Beginning Drivers And Data Center Operators Have In Common

I am starting the process of teaching my 16-year-old daughter to drive a car – pity me! During the countless hours that I've been spending riding around town fearing that at any moment the driving situation that she'll find herself in will exceed her driving abilities, I've had plenty of time to think about one very important concept: risk.

What Does Risk Mean In A Data Center?

The fear that I feel driving with a teenage driver is very similar to the fear that a data center operator feels when they stare at a half-full rack. The big question that is running though their mind is "do I have enough power to this rack left over to allow me to add one more server?" We all use some rule-of-thumb about how many servers can be placed in a rack and once we hit that limit, it's time to start up a new rack.

The end result of all of this "rack risk avoidance" is that more often than not, a modern data center is full of half populated racks. This can mean that there is a lot of waste going on. Clearly there is a lot of space in those half-filled racks that isn't being used. However, there is also left-over electrical energy that is being delivered to the half-filled racks that is also not being used. The end result of all of this is waste: we run out of room in our data centers and we end up purchasing a lot of electricity that we'll never use.

During my time as a student driver instructor I've run into something very similar. When my daughter approaches stopped cars at an intersection, I have her slow down and stop leaving a lot of room between her and the car in front of her. I don't trust her to break hard enough or fast enough to avoid parking my car in the trunk of the car that is sitting at that red light.

The level of risk avoidance that I'm engaging in can be measured in feet: the distance between where I have her stop and the car in front of us. As she becomes a better driver, I'm certain that I'll become more comfortable with her narrowing this gap and stopping the car closer to the one in front of us. Data center operators need to find a way to make the same thing happen in their data centers: they have to find a way to close the gap between a half-full rack and a completely full rack.

How Can Data Center Operators Lower Their Rack Risk?

As a data center operator, if you want to lower your rack risk, then you've got to come up with a way to know more about what's going on in each of the racks in your data center. A great first step is to start to measure how much electricity each rack is using.

There are two different ways to do this: measure energy usage on a per rack basis or measure energy usage on a per outlet basis. Implementing this kind of automated energy usage measuring will provide you with a 24x7x365 view of just how much of the allocated energy is currently being used by the racks in a given server.

Once you know what the peak usage is, you can then more scientifically make a decision about adding another server to the rack. Keep in mind that a server at rest will consume about 120W of electricity and a heavily loaded server could consume 200W or more. Understanding the peak usage of the rack (not just a single server) is critical to making the decision about adding more servers to the rack.

Not all servers are the same. If by using the energy metering features of a PDU you determine that there is a single server that is using the majority of the energy being provided to a rack, then you can move that server to its own rack and then replace it with multiple better behaved servers in order to better fill up the rack. This gives you a chance to make much better use of your limited data center floor space.

No matter if you are talking about how to teach someone to drive or how to make the most of your data center space and power, it's all about finding ways to manage risk.

In the highly competitive data center market, the operator who does the best job of finding a way to minimize their rack risk will be able to maximize their usage of valuable data center real estate and limited power. By doing this they'll be able to offer their customers better prices and more reliable service. Sounds like a risk worth taking!

Hard work does not
guarantee success;
However, success does
not happen
without hard work.

— Dr. Jim Anderson

Photo Credits:

Cover - By: PresidenciaRD
http://www.flickr.com/photos/presidenciard/

Chapter 1 - By: Bob Mical
http://www.flickr.com/photos/small_realm/

Chapter 2 - By: Wikipedia
http://commons.wikimedia.org/wiki/File:SkyControl_PDU.jpg

Chapter 3 - By: Kentaro IEMOTO
http://www.flickr.com/photos/kentaroiemoto/

Chapter 4 - By: Will Hastings
http://www.flickr.com/photos/willsan/

Chapter 5 - By: Jasleen Kaur
http://www.flickr.com/photos/jasleen_kaur/

Chapter 6 - By: Dylan Pankow
http://www.flickr.com/photos/cbcthermal/

Chapter 7 - By: Nick Adams
http://www.flickr.com/photos/personalspokesman/

Chapter 8 - By: Gorazd Božič
http://www.flickr.com/photos/21108040@N06/

Chapter 9 - By: Marc
http://www.flickr.com/photos/sumofmarc/

Chapter 10 - By: get directly down
http://www.flickr.com/photos/65172294@N00/

Chapter 11 - By: Linda
http://www.flickr.com/photos/paneamoreecreativita/

Chapter 12: Patrick Doheny
http://www.flickr.com/photos/14132971@N05/

www.ingramcontent.com/pod-product-compliance
Lightning Source LLC
Chambersburg PA
CBHW061037050326
40689CB00012B/2877